# THE REFINED POET PRESENTS

Poetry Anthology Series

# The Heavens Declare
*
*A Poetical Anthology Extolling Christ's Faithfulness*

**Written by: The Refined Poet**

**The Heavens Declare**
*A Poetical Anthology Extolling Christ's Faithfulness*

All Rights reserved ©2012 by The Refined Poet

*No part of this book may be reproduced or transmitted in any form or by any means, graphic, electronic, or mechanical, including photocopying, recording, taping, or by any information storage or retrieval system, without the permission in writing from the publisher.*

Front & Back Cover Designs by Abundant Truth Publishing
All rights reserved

Abundant Truth Publishing
an imprint of Abundant Truth International Ministries

For information address:
Abundant Truth International
P.O. Box 126
Camden, NC 27921

**Unless otherwise indicated, all of the scripture quotations are taken from the** *Authorized King James Version* **of the Bible. Scripture quotations marked with NIV are taken from the** *New International Version* **of the Bible. Scripture quotations marked with ASV are taken from the** *American Standard Version* **of the Bible. Scripture quotations marked with GW are taken from the** *God's Word Bible.*

ISBN 13: 978-1-60141-406-9

Printed in the United States of America.

# Contents

Preface

Introduction

## Section 1 – Faithful Creator     1

*I Call You Lord*     3
*God Alone*     7
*Your Majesty*     11

## Section 2 – Faithful Guide     15

*The Storm of Self*     17
*Love Her. Hate Her.*     21
*In Need Again*     25

## Section 3 – Faithful Friend     29

*My Strength*     31
*My God*     35
*My All*     39

## Poetical Prayer     43

*Heavenly Father*     45

## Just for Fun     49

# Contents *(cont.)*

*Singing, Sleepy Dave*             *51*

**About the Author**             **55**

**My Poetic Offerings**           **57**

# *Preface*

I hope the poems of this mini anthology will encourage and inspire. I create poetry under the pseudonym of "The Refined Poet" due to the style of my writings.

I do not write from a place of angst, frustration, or inner turmoil. My poetry comes from biblical, thoughtful introspection and consideration of various topics while respecting the many forms of the poetic genre. Hope you enjoy this collection. – TRP

# *Introduction*

Oh, that men would praise the name of Jesus Christ! He demonstrates His love, mercy, and grace daily. The poems in this mini anthology demonstrate, reflect, and express His greatness and faithfulness, inspiring all those in their spiritual walk with Him.

# THE HEAVENS DECLARE
*A Poetical Anthology Extolling Christ's Faithfulness*

-SECTION 1-
# ~Faithful Creator~
*(Poems Declaring His Faithfulness as Lord of All)*

## THE HEAVENS DECLARE
*A Poetical Anthology Extolling Christ's Faithfulness*

***Inspiration:*** *This poetic piece reflects on the rejection and return of Christ. Though He reveals Himself to all, as we experience Him we come to understand His Lord and Savior.*
*~TRP~*

THE HEAVENS DECLARE

*A Poetical Anthology Extolling Christ's Faithfulness*

# ~*I Call You Lord*~
### *(Mark 8:27)*

Though you are mocked by the world,

Defamed as a fraud

Like those in centuries before me,

I call you Lord.

Rejected by your kinsmen,

Ignored by the sons of men

Beaten, committing no offense at all,

I must call you Lord.

Your kingdom was not of this world

It will manifest in glory for all to see

I stand waiting for your reign in majesty

Forever, I will call you Lord

**THE HEAVENS DECLARE**

*A Poetical Anthology Extolling Christ's Faithfulness*

# My Reflections

### THE HEAVENS DECLARE
*A Poetical Anthology Extolling Christ's Faithfulness*

# My Reflections

## THE HEAVENS DECLARE
*A Poetical Anthology Extolling Christ's Faithfulness*

**Inspiration:** This poetic piece reflects on the worthiness of God to receive glory, honor, and power. ~TRP~

THE HEAVENS DECLARE

*A Poetical Anthology Extolling Christ's Faithfulness*

# ~*God Alone*~
*(Psalm 48:1)*

God alone is worthy

to receive the glory.

He alone is worthy

to receive all praise.

God alone is worthy

to receive the honor.

God alone rules in the heaven.

He alone governs the earth.

God alone reigns in the universe.

God alone is worthy.

to receive the honor.

God alone.

# THE HEAVENS DECLARE
*A Poetical Anthology Extolling Christ's Faithfulness*

## My Reflections

_____

_____

_____

_____

_____

_____

_____

_____

_____

_____

_____

_____

_____

_____

# THE HEAVENS DECLARE
*A Poetical Anthology Extolling Christ's Faithfulness*

# My Reflections

_____

_____

_____

_____

_____

_____

_____

_____

_____

_____

_____

_____

_____

_____

_____

# THE HEAVENS DECLARE
*A Poetical Anthology Extolling Christ's Faithfulness*

***Inspiration:*** *This poetic piece expresses the glorious majesty of Jesus Christ. He sits in glory on the right hand of God, the Father.*
*~TRP~*

THE HEAVENS DECLARE

*A Poetical Anthology Extolling Christ's Faithfulness*

# ~*Your Majesty*~
### *(Psalm 104:1)*

*I will praise you O' God,*
*In spirit and truth.*
*Bless your holy name,*
*Bow before you.*
*Great in power and glory.*
*I worship your majesty,*

*I will praise you O' Lord*
*With all of my soul.*
*Exalt your holy name,*
*You have made me whole.*
*Opened my eye,*
*That I may see.*
*I worship your majesty.*

## THE HEAVENS DECLARE
*A Poetical Anthology Extolling Christ's Faithfulness*

***G****reat in power.*

*Great in strength.*

*Maker of all,*

*Creator of everything.*

*Great in splendor and glory,*

*I worship your majesty,*

## THE HEAVENS DECLARE
*A Poetical Anthology Extolling Christ's Faithfulness*

# My Reflections

_____

_____

_____

_____

_____

_____

_____

_____

_____

_____

_____

_____

_____

_____

_____

_____

_____

## My Reflections

THE HEAVENS DECLARE
*A Poetical Anthology Extolling Christ's Faithfulness*

-SECTION 2-
# ~Faithful Guide~
*(Poems of His Faithfulness in Personal Distress/Temptations)*

# THE HEAVENS DECLARE

*A Poetical Anthology Extolling Christ's Faithfulness*

**Inspiration:** *This poetic piece demonstrates the inner struggles that one can have while following Christ. Paul alluded to this inner struggle to do what is right in his writings. Based upon Romans 7:21 ~TRP~*

THE HEAVENS DECLARE

*A Poetical Anthology Extolling Christ's Faithfulness*

# ~*The Storm of Self*~

*My God, here it is again!*
*I see the dark clouds of my thoughts forming.*
*Your brightness is hid from my eyes.*
*The endless rains of tears burst down my face.*
*Billows and waves of emotions crash about me.*
*Again, I am lost in the storm of self.*

*My two adversaries box me in.*
*The enemy of self says, "Quit!*
*You can't make it!*
*You don't want to do better!*
*You will never overcome!"*

*The evil one whispers so cunningly,*

# THE HEAVENS DECLARE
*A Poetical Anthology Extolling Christ's Faithfulness*

*"Where is your God?*
*He does not care about you!*
*God won't help, forgive, or hear you!"*
*The storm of self has turned into a*
*typhoon of despair.*
*In the midst of the storm,*
*Your life boat appears.*
*A psalm, a hymn, a word,*
*Calming the fiercest winds of the soul.*
*Praise from my mouth springs forth;*
*as a gentle breeze.*
*Your love floods my being;*
*like golden rays of the sun.*

*The storm of self may come again.*
*But your love and faithfulness will restore,*
*Restore my soul, peace, and joy.*
*I will make it through self and behold the*
*Savior.*

## My Reflections

# THE HEAVENS DECLARE
*A Poetical Anthology Extolling Christ's Faithfulness*

***Inspiration:*** *This poetic piece describes dangers of falling in love with money. Christ will be faithful to help us guard against its allure. We need money in this world, but we must not love it and allow the pursuit of it to dominate our lives. ~TRP~*

THE HEAVENS DECLARE

*A Poetical Anthology Extolling Christ's Faithfulness*

# *~Love Her. Hate Her.~*
### *(I Timothy 6:10)*

*Love her and she will destroy you.*
*Disown her and you will come to ruin.*
*Treasure her for her worth,*
*Avoid the snare of her desire.*

*She holds men and women alike,*
*None can escape her allure.*
*Kill for her, work for her,*
*Do what you will.*
*All who are controlled by her,*
*Their lives will surely become destitute.*

*She attracts indiscriminately.*
*She allures without remorse.*
*Her absence makes men miserable.*
*Her presence is bitter-sweet.*

# THE HEAVENS DECLARE
*A Poetical Anthology Extolling Christ's Faithfulness*

*What can be said of this woman*
*Who is adored worldwide?*
*With her is pain and pleasure,*
*Joy and sorrow are her rewards.*

*Treasure her for her worth,*
*Avoid the snare of her desire.*
*Love Her. Hate Her.*
*Money is here to stay.*

**THE HEAVENS DECLARE**

*A Poetical Anthology Extolling Christ's Faithfulness*

# My Reflections

# THE HEAVENS DECLARE
*A Poetical Anthology Extolling Christ's Faithfulness*

***Inspiration:*** *This poetic piece reflects the need for confession and repentance in the Christian life. Though we are made righteous by faith, we must recognize areas of sin and weakness, turning from them and laying them down before Christ. He will guide in the path of righteousness. ~TRP~*

## ~*In Need Again*~
### *(Psalm 51:2)*

*I know I don't deserve,*

*All of your grace.*

*I know I don't deserve,*

*All of your mercy.*

*Before you O' Lord,*

*I do stand.*

*I am in need again.*

*Take away my sin*

*Soothe my troubled mind*

*Wash me clean*

*Make me whole*

*I am in need again.*

# THE HEAVENS DECLARE
*A Poetical Anthology Extolling Christ's Faithfulness*

# My Reflections

## THE HEAVENS DECLARE
*A Poetical Anthology Extolling Christ's Faithfulness*

# My Reflections

# THE HEAVENS DECLARE
*A Poetical Anthology Extolling Christ's Faithfulness*

THE HEAVENS DECLARE

*A Poetical Anthology Extolling Christ's Faithfulness*

-SECTION 3-
# ~Faithful Friend~
*(Poems Expressing His Personal Presence in our Lives)*

# THE HEAVENS DECLARE
*A Poetical Anthology Extolling Christ's Faithfulness*

***Inspiration:*** *This poetic piece declares the Christian's need for Christ presence and strength daily. He will provide all that is necessary for success. ~TRP~*

## ~My Strength~
*(Isaiah 12:2-3)*

*In the wilderness*
*His presence moved with the tabernacle*
*In the land of Canaan*
*His presence dwelt in the Temple*
*In this time*
*His presence lives in men*

*I have witnessed His power*
*Felt His embrace*
*Moving me from sin*
*To become a holy dwelling place*
*Full of peace, joy, and hope,*
*Proclaiming the good news of His love*

*My heart is His tabernacle,*
*Moved by His sway*
*My body is His temple,*

*Unmoved from the faith*

*His Spirit convicts and comforts*

*His presence guides and protects*

*Once given over to sin*

*Set apart for disgrace*

*His presence now within me*

*Filling every place*

*What a wonderful change in me*

*My Strength,*

*The Holy Spirit in the temple that is me*

## THE HEAVENS DECLARE
*A Poetical Anthology Extolling Christ's Faithfulness*

# My Reflections

# THE HEAVENS DECLARE
*A Poetical Anthology Extolling Christ's Faithfulness*

***Inspiration:*** *This poetic piece expresses the personal relationship with have with God through Christ. He is personally involved in our daily lives. No one compares to Him in this life. ~TRP~*

THE HEAVENS DECLARE

*A Poetical Anthology Extolling Christ's Faithfulness*

# ~*My God*~
*(Psalm 72:18)*

*There are not enough words to describe*
*The greatness of my God*
*No adjectives effectively communicate*
*The ways of Him possessing power to create*
*If you can, please tell me,*
*What words can describe my God faithfully!*

*My God is better than good*
*He is greater than the greatest*
*Demonstrating love and kindness*
*In a world covered in spiritual blindness*
*Extending mercy to thousands*
*All creation must laud Him*
*For He is mighty*

## THE HEAVENS DECLARE
*A Poetical Anthology Extolling Christ's Faithfulness*

**M**y God is Lord of all
*He comforts when I fall*
*I call upon His name*
*It is worthy to be praised*
*Yes, My God is God*

## THE HEAVENS DECLARE
*A Poetical Anthology Extolling Christ's Faithfulness*

# My Reflections

# THE HEAVENS DECLARE
*A Poetical Anthology Extolling Christ's Faithfulness*

***Inspiration:*** *This poetic piece establishes the fact that Christ is our all. Though we exist, it is because of His infinite love and mercy. He is our shepherd and daily guide. ~TRP~*

THE HEAVENS DECLARE

*A Poetical Anthology Extolling Christ's Faithfulness*

## ~*My All*~
### *(Psalm 23:1)*

The Lord is my shepherd
I shall not want.
The Creator is my shield,
Whom shall I fear?
The God of gods is my peace,
He gives me sweet rest
He is my all

The Comforter is my friend,
How can I feel alone?
The Compass is my guide
I'm never lost, safe in His arms
The Crutch is my strength
I won't fail or fall
He is my all

*Jesus is my all*

*He will answer when I call*

*Times when I feel alone,*

*Overshadowed by the safety of His arms*

*The Lord is my all*

*Jesus is my all*

*He truly is my all*

# My Reflections

# THE HEAVENS DECLARE
*A Poetical Anthology Extolling Christ's Faithfulness*

# My Reflections

THE HEAVENS DECLARE

*A Poetical Anthology Extolling Christ's Faithfulness*

# *Poetical Prayer*

## THE HEAVENS DECLARE
*A Poetical Anthology Extolling Christ's Faithfulness*

***Inspiration:*** *I wrote this poetic prayer while considering family, friends, and others who were in need of prayer.*
*Personally… a heartfelt write.*
*~TRP~*

THE HEAVENS DECLARE

*A Poetical Anthology Extolling Christ's Faithfulness*

# ~*Heavenly Father*~
### *(Matthew 6:9)*

*I come before you now,*
*Through and by Jesus Christ.*
*Asking you to move in the life of my family*
*And those who have given you their lives.*

***S**trengthen now by your grace*
*Their needs are many,*
*Let their concerns be before your face.*
*Establish their hearts in peace, finishing the race.*

***Y**ou provided for Israel in the wilderness*
*And protected Daniel in the lion's den.*
*Let the sad be comforted by your tenderness,*
*Forgive them for all of their sins.*

The Refined Poet

# THE HEAVENS DECLARE
*A Poetical Anthology Extolling Christ's Faithfulness*

***I** thank you now that you are faithful.*
*In advance, I bless you for I am grateful.*
*You will bless the many needs of my family,*
*Demonstrating your grace, power, and love to all.*

***I** stand in expectation now of your blessing,*
*We will always rejoice in your acts of love.*
*I bless you as always, wanting your will to be done,*
*Ever looking for the return of your Son.*
***I**n the name of Jesus Christ I pray.* **AMEN**

# My Reflections

## THE HEAVENS DECLARE
*A Poetical Anthology Extolling Christ's Faithfulness*

# My Reflections

# THE HEAVENS DECLARE
*A Poetical Anthology Extolling Christ's Faithfulness*

## *Just for Fun*

# THE HEAVENS DECLARE
*A Poetical Anthology Extolling Christ's Faithfulness*

***Inspiration:*** *Poem written for personal enjoyment. Hope you like it. ~TRP~*

THE HEAVENS DECLARE

*A Poetical Anthology Extolling Christ's Faithfulness*

## Singing, Sleepy Dave

*Dave stood before the crowd singing,*
*His song told a story, having deep meaning.*

*No one expected what happened next.*
*Eyes looked upon him confused and perplexed.*

*For, Dave nodded and slept in the middle of the song.*
*He didn't respond as the music continued to play along.*

*Then all of sudden without missing a beat;*
*He awakened to finish his song and returned to his seat.*

# THE HEAVENS DECLARE
*A Poetical Anthology Extolling Christ's Faithfulness*

# THE HEAVENS DECLARE
*A Poetical Anthology Extolling Christ's Faithfulness*

## My Reflections

**THE HEAVENS DECLARE**
*A Poetical Anthology Extolling Christ's Faithfulness*

# My Reflections

# ~About the Author~

The Refined Poet is a poet, psalmist, author, and minister. He has written numerous poems, books, articles, blogs, teaching resources, devotional materials, and music for the Christian community.

His poetry reflects sound, biblical Christian thought, encouraging those of the Christian faith. His versatility in poetic prose provides inspiration for those who appreciate the poetry genre. His motto for his poetry is: "Write to Inspire. Write to Express. Write to Live."

I create poetry under the pseudonym of "The Refined Poet" due to the style of my writings. I do not write from a place of angst, frustration, or inner turmoil. My poetry comes from biblical, thoughtful introspection and consideration of various topics while respecting the many forms of the poetic genre. ~TRP~

## THE HEAVENS DECLARE
*A Poetical Anthology Extolling Christ's Faithfulness*

For more poetry, please visit The Refined Poet online at therefinedpoet.net

# THE HEAVENS DECLARE
*A Poetical Anthology Extolling Christ's Faithfulness*

# My Poetic Offerings

**THE HEAVENS DECLARE**

*A Poetical Anthology Extolling Christ's Faithfulness*

# "In this section, I invite you to try creating some poetry of your own."

## THE HEAVENS DECLARE
*A Poetical Anthology Extolling Christ's Faithfulness*

# My Poetic Offering

_____

_____

_____

_____

_____

_____

_____

_____

_____

_____

_____

_____

_____

_____

_____

_____

## THE HEAVENS DECLARE
*A Poetical Anthology Extolling Christ's Faithfulness*

# My Poetic Offering

# THE HEAVENS DECLARE
*A Poetical Anthology Extolling Christ's Faithfulness*

## My Poetic Offering

# THE HEAVENS DECLARE
*A Poetical Anthology Extolling Christ's Faithfulness*

## My Poetic Offering

_____

_____

_____

_____

_____

_____

_____

_____

_____

_____

_____

_____

_____

_____

_____

**THE HEAVENS DECLARE**

*A Poetical Anthology Extolling Christ's Faithfulness*

# My Poetic Offering

**THE HEAVENS DECLARE**
*A Poetical Anthology Extolling Christ's Faithfulness*

# My Poetic Offering

## THE HEAVENS DECLARE
*A Poetical Anthology Extolling Christ's Faithfulness*

# My Poetic Offering

**THE HEAVENS DECLARE**

*A Poetical Anthology Extolling Christ's Faithfulness*

# My Poetic Offering

www.ingramcontent.com/pod-product-compliance
Lightning Source LLC
Chambersburg PA
CBHW050344010526
44119CB00049B/691